Simple Mitts

One set (4) size 5 (3.75mm) double-pointed needles (dpns) *or size to obtain gauge*

Notions

- Stitch marker

Size

Sized for Adult Woman.

Measurements

- **Length** 10½"/26.5cm
- **Hand circumference** 7"/18cm

Gauge

24 sts and 36 rnds to 4"/10cm over St st using size 5 (3.75mm) needles.
Take time to check gauge.

Mitt

(make 2)
Cast on 42 sts. Join, taking care not to twist sts. Place marker for beg of rnd. P 1 rnd, k 1 rnd, p 1 rnd, then work in St st (k every rnd) until piece measures 7½"/19cm from beg.

Thumb opening

Note Thumb opening is created by working back and forth in rows on all sts.
Next row (RS) Knit to marker, turn.
Next row (WS) Purl.
Rep last 2 rows until thumb opening measures 1½"/4cm.

Hand

Next rnd K to marker, do not turn, rejoin rnd and cont in St st for 1"/2.5cm.
P 1 rnd, k 1 rnd, p 1 rnd. Bind off.

Thumb

Pick up and k 16 sts around thumb opening. Join and pm for beg of rnd. K 5 rnds. P 1 rnd, k 1 rnd, p 1 rnd. Bind off. ■

Eyelet Rib Wristlets

Yarn (3)

- 117yd/107m, 1¾oz/50g of any DK weight wool/acrylic/nylon yarn

Needles

- One pair size 6 (4mm) needles *or size to obtain gauge*

Size

Sized for Adult Woman.

Measurements

- **Circumference** (unstretched) 5"/12.5cm
- **Length** 6"/15.5cm

Gauge

26 sts and 28 rows to 4"/10cm over eyelet rib using size 6 (4mm) needles.
Take time to check gauge.

Eyelet Rib

(multiple of 6 sts plus 3)
Row 1 (RS) K1 (selvage st), k1, *yo, k1, k3tog, k1, yo, k1; rep from *, end k1 (selvage st).
Row 2 P1 (selvage st), p1, *k5, p1; rep from *, end p1 (selvage st).
Rep rows 1 and 2 for eyelet rib.

Wristlet

Cast on 33 sts.
Row 1 (RS) P1, *k1, p1; rep from * to end.
Cont in k1, p1 rib as established for 3 rows more.
Work in eyelet rib until piece measures 5½"/14cm from beg, end with a WS row.
Next row (RS) P1, *k1, p1; rep from * to end. Cont in k1, p1 rib as established for 3 rows more.
Bind off in rib.

Finishing

Fold wristlet in half lengthwise. Beg at lower edge, sew side seam for 3½"/9cm, leave next 1"/2.5cm unsewn for thumb opening, sew rem 1½"/4cm to close wristlet. ■

style tip

While these wristlets are cute and cropped, you can easily make them longer. Try them mid-length in white for a spring wedding, or to the elbow in black for evening!

Fingerless Mitts

Yarn

- 190yd/174m, 4oz/113g of any worsted weight wool yarn in blue

Needles

- One set (5) size 4 (3.5mm) double-pointed needles (dpns) *or size to obtain gauge*

Notions

- Stitch markers
- Scrap yarn

Size

Sized for Adult Woman.

Measurements

- **Wrist circumference** 8"/20.5cm
- **Length** 9"/23cm

Gauge

20 sts and 32 rnds to 4"/10cm over St st using size 4 (3.5mm) needles.

Take time to check gauge.

Double Broken Rib

(multiple of 4 sts)

Rnds 1 and 2 *K2, p2; rep from * around.

Rnd 3 Knit.

Rnd 4 Purl.

Rep rnds 1–4 for double broken rib.

Offset Broken Rib

(multiple of 4 sts)

Rnds 1 and 2 K1, *p2, k2; rep from * to last 3 sts, p2, k1.

Rnd 3 Knit.

Rnd 4 Purl.

Rnds 5 and 6 P1, *k2, p2; rep from * to last 3 sts, k2, p1.

Rnd 7 Knit.

Rnd 8 Purl.

Rep rnds 1–8 for offset broken rib.

Right Mitt

Cast on 40 sts and divide evenly over 4 dpns (10 sts on each needle). Join, taking care not to twist sts, and place marker (pm) for beg of rnd.

Work in double broken rib until piece measures 4"/10cm from beg, end with a rnd 4.

Hand

Next rnd K9, work rnd 1 of offset broken rib over next 20 sts, k to end of rnd.

Cont in this manner until 8 rnds of offset rib pat are complete.

Thumb gusset

Next (inc) rnd Cont in pat as established to last 10 sts, pm, M1, k1, M1, pm, k to end of rnd—42 sts.

Work one rnd even.

Next (inc) rnd Work to first gusset marker, sl marker, M1, knit to next marker, M1, sl marker, work to end of rnd—44 sts.

Rep inc rnd every other rnd 5 times more—15 sts between gusset markers.

Next rnd Work to first gusset marker, place next 15 sts on scrap yarn for thumb, cast on 3 sts, work to end of rnd—42 sts.

Work even until piece measures 9"/23cm from beg, end with a row 3 or 7. Bind off purlwise.

Thumb

Place the 15 thumb sts on 2 dpn. Rejoin yarn and with 3rd dpn, pick up and k 5 sts along thumb opening, k15. Pm for beg of rnd. Work 3 rnds in St st (k every rnd).

Next (dec) rnd Ssk, k1, k2tog, k to end of rnd—18 sts. Work 5 rnds even. Bind off purlwise.

Left Mitt

Work same as for right mitt to thumb gusset.

Thumb gusset

K7, pm, M1, k1, M1, pm, cont in pat as established. Complete as for right mitt. ■

style tip

If you prefer fitted fingers, use a tapestry needle and some extra yarn to join the front and back together between each finger.

Arm Warmers

Yarn (4)

- 115yd/105m, 1¾oz/50g of any worsted weight wool yarn in blue

Needles

- One set (4) double-pointed needles (dpns) each sizes 4 and 5 (3.5 and 3.75mm) *or size to obtain gauge*

Notions

- Stitch markers
- Cable needle (cn)

Measurements

- **Cuff circumference** 9"/23cm
- **Length** 14½"/37cm

Gauge

24 sts and 30 rows/rnds to 4"/10cm over k2, p2 rib using larger needles.
Take time to check gauge.

Stitch Glossary

10-st LC Sl 5 sts to cn and hold to front, k5, k5 from cn.

Right Arm Warmer

With smaller needles, cast on 52 sts and divide on 3 dpns as foll: Dpn #1 (palm side) 13 sts; dpn #2 (palm side) 13 sts; dpn #3 (back of hand) 26 sts. Place marker (pm) and join, taking care not to twist sts.

Rnd 1 On dpn #1, [P2, k2] 3 times, p1; on dpn #2, p1, [k2, p2] 3 times; on dpn #3, k2, [p2, k2] 6 times.

Cont in k2, p2 rib for 3"/7.5cm. Change to larger needles.

Rnd 1 On dpn #1, rib 13 sts; on dpn #2, rib 13 sts; on dpn #3, rib 8 sts, k10, rib 8 sts.

Rnds 2–11 Rep rnd 1.

Cable rnd 12 Rib to the 10-st center rib, work 10-st LC , rib to end of rnd.

Rep last 12 rnds until piece measures 4½"/11.5cm from beg.

Dec rnd On dpn #1, rib 6, SKP, rib to end; on dpn #2, rib to last 8 sts, k2tog, rib to end; on dpn #3, work even.

Rep dec rnd every 6th rnd 3 times more—9 sts on dpn #1, 9 sts on dpn #2, 26 sts on dpn #3; 44 sts total. Work even until piece measures 11½"/29cm from beg.

Thumb opening

Next row Work to end of rnd, turn.

Work back and forth in rows for 1½"/4cm. Change to smaller needles, rejoin and work in rnds for 2"/5cm more. Bind off.

Thumb

With smaller needle, pick up and k 18 sts around thumb opening. Divide sts evenly onto 3 needles and join, pm to mark beg of rnd. K 2 rnds. Then work 2 rnds in k1, p1 rib. Bind off in rib.

Left Arm Warmer

Work same as right arm warmer to thumb opening. Remove marker, work next 18 sts, pm for new beg of rnd, turn. Complete as for right arm warmer. ■

Lacy Fingerless Gloves

Yarn (1)

- 175yd/160m, 1¾oz/50g of any fingering weight wool yarn in mint green

Needles

- One pair size 4 (3.5mm) needles *or size to obtain gauge*

Measurements

- Approx 3½ x 4"/9 x 10cm

Gauge

24 sts and 36 rows to 4"/10cm over St st using size 4 (3.5mm) needles.

Take time to check gauge.

Wrister

(make 2)

Cast on 41 sts. K 3 rows.

Beg with a WS row, work 9 rows in St st (k on RS, p on WS).

Beg chart

Next row (RS) Work row 1 of chart to rep line, work 10-st rep 4 times.

Cont to foll chart in this way through row 14.

Beg with a RS row, work 10 rows in St st.

K 3 rows. Bind off.

Finishing

Sew side seams from top and bottom edges along garter and St st rows only, leaving chart rows unseamed for thumb opening. ■

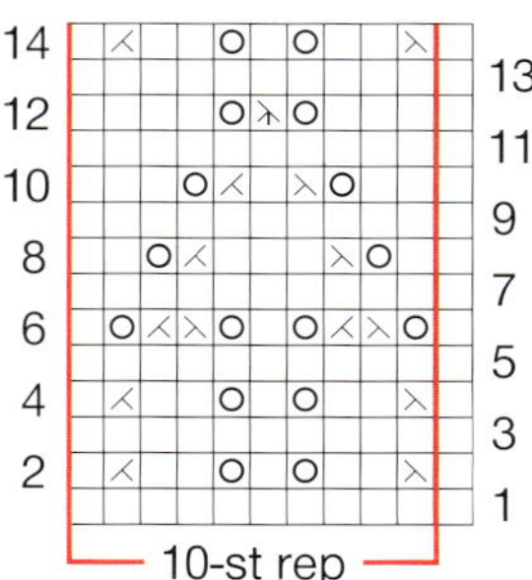

STITCH KEY

- ☐ k on RS, p on WS
- k2tog
- ssk
- yo
- SK2P

Shell Rib Wristlets

Yarn (3)

- 228yd/208m, 3½oz/100g of any DK weight wool yarn in blue multi

Needles

- One pair size 6 (4mm) needles *or size to obtain gauge*

Size

Sized for Adult Woman.

Measurements

- **Circumference** (unstretched) 6"/15cm
- **Length** 9"/23cm

Gauge

21 sts and 30 rows to 4"/10cm over shell rib using size 6 (4mm) needles.

Take time to check gauge.

Shell Rib

(beg with multiple of 7 sts plus 2)

Row 1 (WS) P2, *k1, [yo, k1] 4 times, p2; rep from * to end—multiple is now 11 sts plus 2.

Row 2 K2, *p1, [k1, p1] 4 times, k2; rep from * to end.

Row 3 P2, *k1, p1, ssk, k1, k2tog, p1, k1, p2; rep from * to end.

Row 4 K2, *p1, k1, p3tog, k1, p1, k2; rep from * to end—multiple is back to 7 sts plus 2.

Rep rows 1–4 for shell rib.

Wristlet

Cast on 30 sts. Work in shell rib for 9"/23cm, end with a WS row.

Bind off loosely.

Finishing

Fold wristlet in half lengthwise. Beg at lower edge, sew side seam for 6½"/16.5cm, leave next 1"/2.5cm unsewn for thumb opening, sew rem 1½"/4cm to close wristlet. ■

Leaf-Rib Wristlets

Yarn
- 270yd/247m, 3½oz/100g of any sportweight wool/acrylic yarn in blue muti

Needles
- One pair size 4 (3.5mm) needles *or size to obtain gauge*

Size
Sized for Adult Woman.

Measurements
- **Circumference** (unstretched) 6¾"/17cm
- **Length** 10"/25.5cm

Gauge
20 sts and 28 rows to 4"/10cm over leaf rib using size 4 (3.5mm) needles.

Take time to check gauge.

Leaf Rib
(multiple of 6 sts plus 4)

Rows 1 and 3 (WS) Purl.

Row 2 (RS) K2, *k3, yo, SK2P, yo; rep from *, to last 2 sts, k2.

Row 4 K2, *yo, SK2P, yo, k3; rep from * to last 2 sts, k2.

Rep rows 1–4 for leaf rib.

Wristlet
Cast on 34 sts using picot cast on as foll: *Cast on 6 sts, bind off 2 sts; rep from *, end cast on 2 sts. Knit 1 row, purl 1 row, knit 1 row.

Work in leaf rib until piece measures 10"/25.5cm from beg, end with a WS row.

Bind off loosely.

Finishing
Fold wristlet in half lengthwise. Beg at lower edge, sew side seam for 7½"/19cm, leave next 1"/2.5cm unsewn for thumb opening, sew rem 1½"/4cm to close wristlet. ■

Lace Mitts

Yarn

- 200yd/183m, 2oz/57g of any sport weight wool yarn in variegated blue

Needles

- One set (5) size 4 (3.5mm) double-pointed needles (dpns) *or size to obtain gauge*

Notions

- Stitch markers
- Scrap yarn

Sizes

Sized for Small and Large. Shown in size Small.

Measurements

- **Hand circumference** 7½ (8½)"/19(21.5)cm
- **Length** 8"/20.5cm

Gauge

26 sts and 36 rnds to 4"/10cm over lace pat using size 4 (3.5mm) needles.
Take time to check gauge.

Lace Pattern

(multiple of 8 sts)

Rnd 1 [Yo, ssk, k3, k2tog, yo, k1] 6 (7) times.
Rnd 2 (and all even numbered rnds) Knit.
Rnd 3 [K1, yo, ssk, k1, k2tog, yo, k2] 6 (7) times.
Rnd 5 Rep rnd 1.
Rnd 7 Rep rnd 3.
Rnd 9 [K2, yo, S2KP, yo, k3] 6 (7) times.
Rnd 11 [K2tog, yo, k3, yo, ssk, k1] 6 (7) times.
Rnd 13 Slip first st to end of rnd, pm for new beg of rnd, [yo, k5, yo, S2KP] 6 (7) times.
Rnd 15 [K1, k2tog, yo, k1, yo, ssk, k2] 6 (7) times.
Rnd 17 [K2tog, yo, k3, yo, ssk, k1] 6 (7) times.
Rnd 19 Rep rnd 13.
Rnd 20 Knit.

Mitts

Cast on 48 (56) sts. Join, taking care not to twist sts, and place marker (pm) for beg of rnd.
Next rnd *K1, p1; rep from * to end.
Rep this rnd for k1, p1 rib 3 times more.

Beg lace pat

Work 8-st rep 6 (7) times around until rnd 10 is complete. Rep rnds 9 and 10 twelve times more, then rnd 9 once. Piece measures approx 4¼"/11cm from beg.

Gusset

Next rnd K2, pm for thumb, k3, pm for thumb, k3, knit to end of rnd.
Next (inc) rnd K2, sl marker, yo, k to next marker, yo, sl marker, k3, foll rnd 9 of pat, work 8-st rep 5 (6) times over rem 40 (48) sts—5 thumb sts.
Next rnd Foll rnd 10 of lace pat.
Rep last 2 rnds 6 times more—17 thumb sts.
Next rnd K2, removing thumb markers, place next 17 sts on scrap yarn for thumb, cast on 3 sts, k3, foll rnd 9 of chart, work 8-st rep 5 (6) times over rem 40 (48) sts—48 (56) sts in rnd.
Next rnd Knit.

Hand

Work rnds 11–20, then rep rnds 15–20 once more.
Next rnd *K1, p1; rep from * to end.
Rep last rnd once more. Bind off in pat.

Thumb

Place 17 thumb sts on needles.
With RS facing, rejoin yarn and pick up and k 3 sts along cast-on edge of thumb opening, pm for beg of rnd—20 sts.
Next rnd *K1, p1; rep from * to end. Rep this rnd 6 times more. Bind off in pat. ■

Cabled Wristers

Yarn (4)

- 208yd/190m, 3½oz/100g of any worsted weight wool yarn in gold

Needles

- One pair size 7 (4.5mm) needles *or size to obtain gauge*

Notions

- Cable needle (cn)
- Ten ½"/12mm buttons

Size

Sized for Adult Woman.

Measurements

- **Circumference** (buttoned) 7½"/19cm
- **Length** (wrist to fingers) 7"/18cm

Gauge

20 sts and 35 rows to 4"/10cm over garter st using size 7 (4.5mm) needles.
Take time to check gauge.

Stitch Glossary

4-st RC Sl 2 sts to cn and hold to *back*, k2, k2 from cn.

4-st LC Sl 2 sts to cn and hold to *front*, k2, k2 from cn.

Left Wrister

With size 7 (4.5mm) needles, cast on 35 sts. Knit 2 rows.

Next (buttonhole) row (WS) K3, [yo, k2tog, k5] 4 times, yo, k2tog, k2.

Knit 2 rows.

Beg back of hand

Row 1 (RS) K10 for wristband, p2, [k4, p2] 3 times, k5.

Rows 2 and 4 K7, [p4, k2] 3 times, k10.

Row 3 K10, p2, [4-st RC, p2] 3 times, k5.

Rows 5 and 6 Rep rows 1 and 2.

Rep rows 1–6 four times more, then rep rows 1–5 once more. Knit 1 row.

Thumb opening

Next row (RS) K12, bind off 10 sts, k to end.

Next row K13, cast on 10 sts over bound-off sts, k to end.

Palm

Work in garter st (k every row) until piece measures 3½"/9cm from thumb opening. Bind off.

Right Wrister

Cast on and work as for Left Wrister, end with buttonhole row.

Beg back of hand

Row 1 (RS) K5, p2, [k4, p2] 3 times, k10 for wristband.

Rows 2 and 4 K12, [p4, k2] 3 times, k5.

Row 3 K5, p2, [4-st LC, p2] 3 times, k10.

Rows 5 and 6 Rep rows 1 and 2.

Rep rows 1–6 four times more, then rep rows 1–5 once more. Knit 1 row.

Thumb opening

Next row (RS) K13, bind off 10 sts, k to end of row.

Next row K12, cast on 10 sts over bound-off sts, k to end.

Palm

Work as for Left Wrister.

Finishing

Sew on buttons opposite buttonholes. ■

Ruffled Wristers

Yarn

- 153yd/140m, 1oz/30g of any DK weight wool/cotton yarn in light blue

Needles

- One set (5) size 5 (3.75mm) double-pointed needles (dpns) *or size to obtain gauge*

Size

Sized for Adult Woman.

Measurements

- **Circumference** Approx 6"/15cm, (will stretch to fit up to 9"/23cm)
- **Length** 6"/15cm

Gauge

26 sts and 34 rows to 4"/10cm over lace chart using size 5 (3.75mm) needles.
Take time to check gauge.

Wristers

Ruffle

With dpns, cast on 80 sts. Divide sts evenly over 4 dpns (20 sts on dpn). Place marker (pm) and join, being careful not to twist sts. P 1 rnd, k 4 rnds.

Next rnd *K2tog; rep from * around—40 sts.

Beg chart

Rnd 1 Work 20-st rep chart 2 times around. When 28 rnds of chart pat are complete, work rnds 1–14 once more. Work in k1, p1 rib for 4 rnds. Bind off loosely in rib. ■

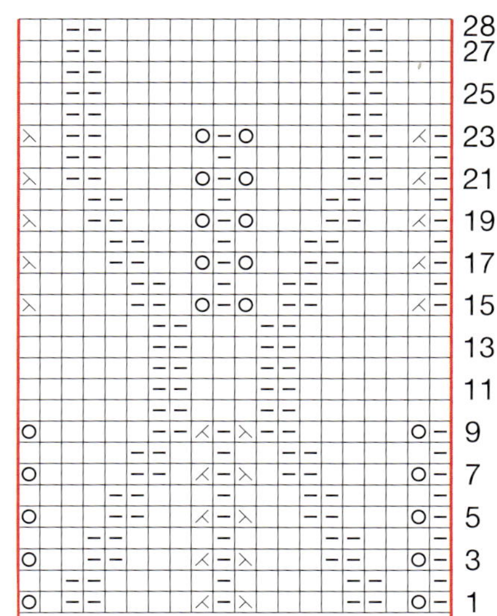

STITCH KEY

- ☐ k on RS
- ⊟ p on RS
- ⊙ yo
- ⧄ k2tog
- ⧅ ssk